MW01491247

Golf By the Books

Christian Devotionals

Cover Photo: Harry Underwood

Golf by The Books

Christian Devotionals

Harry Underwood

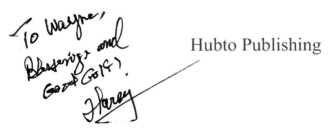
To Wayne,
Blessings and
Good Golf!
Harry

Hubto Publishing

No part of this book may be reproduced, stored in a retrieval system, or transmitted by any means without written permission of the author.

© 2013 Harry Underwood. All rights reserved.

ISBN: 978-0-9883776-0-8

Published by Hubto Publishing, Winston-Salem, NC

Biblical quotations are from The New Revised Standard Version Bible, © 1989 by the Division of Christian Education of the National Council of Churches in the U.S.A., and are used by permission.

"For there is no distinction, since all have sinned and fall short of the glory of God; they are now justified by his grace as a gift, through the redemption that is in Jesus Christ whom God put forward as a sacrifice of atonement by his blood, effective through faith."
Romans 3:22b-25a

Table of Contents

3

Preface

Chaos occurs when everyone plays by his or her own rules. Golf is many things but not chaos. One reason for golf's popularity is because it is played by standard rules based on fair play that accommodate golfers of all skill levels. It is a game played by the book, *The Rules of Golf*, published by the United States Golf Association (USGA). When USGA golf rules originated in 1895 there were only 13. In 2012, there are 34 rules contained in a pocket-sized book of 182 pages.

To be equitable and fun for all participants, every game or sport has its set of rules. Team sports have referees and umpires to enforce their rules. In the sport of golf, the golfers must enforce the rules themselves. If a golfer does not consistently follow the rules, he will soon find that he is playing by himself. He may have found the only person who will enjoy playing with him.

Life, also, must have something to guide behavior and the interaction of people with each other. We can live by following one of many religious or humanistic philosophies. But, many believe that the best guide for a satisfying life, eternally, is one grounded in the Word of God. The Creator has chosen to provide,

4

through divine inspiration, magnificent insight into God, mankind and the relationship between the two. It is found in a book, the Bible, which is composed of the Hebrew Scriptures (Old Testament) and the New Testament.

Golf By the Books is for golfers, spouses of golfers and people who would like to learn more about the game. This collection of devotionals connects the USGA's *The Rules of Golf* with the Bible, God's biblical rules of living. It links concepts about, actions in, and observations around the game of golf to life lessons grounded in the Holy Scriptures through the use of comparisons, observations and illustrations.

After reading and meditating on these devotionals, the reader will gain different insights into golf, golfers, God and the Bible. The author's desire is that they will contribute to more satisfying experiences on the golf course and a more fulfilling Christian life. Read these devotionals with joy and hope.

The Game

A Never-ending Challenge

On a bright, sunny morning, I stand on the manicured tee preparing to drive my first ball of the day. The seductive lure of this game draws me back again to enjoy the round with hopes of bettering my previous performances and winning against my opponents and the course.

Conceptually, golf is simple. Just take the fewest strokes necessary to drop a little white ball into a four-and-one-quarter-inch hole. In performance, golf is complex. Simply striking the ball toward the cup is impeded by the design of the course, the weather, the opponents, and, significantly, by the golfers themselves. One good shot may immediately be followed by an errant one. Seldom does everything go as planned and we are challenged.

Like golf, life is both simple and complex. Sometimes, it involves just living on a day by day basis without exertion. At other times great effort must be expended to develop goals, employ complex strategies and pursue them with intense dedication. Sometimes, there are major obstacles to overcome.

For Christians, life's goal is simple. It is not about achieving the lowest or highest score, but about finding and pleasing God, who redeems us from our sins. Jesus said that whoever believes in him may have eternal life (John 3:15).

We begin by accepting Jesus Christ as our Savior and showing our gratitude by living our lives in a manner pleasing to God. Be like the brother of Jesus, "I by my works will show you my faith" (James 2:18b). This means, once accepting Jesus, performing acts of love towards God and our neighbors.

We will never achieve perfection in golf or in life. Nonetheless, in the sport and in our daily living, we can focus on our goals, overcome our challenges and do our best while we appreciate the opportunities we have been given. Let us give thanks to God.

"Pursue righteousness, godliness, faith, love, endurance, gentleness. Fight the good fight of the faith: take hold of the eternal life, to which you were called." 1 Timothy 6:11b-12a

Establishing Par

My golf goal, at least my fantasy, is to shoot a round at par. In a typical game, I par several holes, but to do so for all eighteen seems quite impossible for me. I like to think, maybe, the problem is with established par, instead of with me.

The United States Golf Association course rating for par used worldwide is a numerical value applied to each set of tees at a particular golf course establishing the number of strokes it should take for a good amateur (scratch) golfer to play the course.

Par is determined primarily by the length of each hole from the tee to the pin. Par-three holes range between 100 and 250 yards, par-four holes between 250 and 450 yards and par-five holes between 450 and 600 yards. The terrain and obstacles (like trees, bunkers, water and hills), all of which that may require a golfer to use more or less strokes, influence par. Most golf courses have par values of 72, comprised of four par-threes, ten par-fours, and four par-fives.

In the game of life, par is set by God. To live up to par is to live in accordance with the laws, commandments and precepts of the Lord. Jesus condensed them to loving God with all your heart, soul and mind and loving your neighbor (both partners and competitors) as yourself. Doing so leads to a life of righteousness and great reward.

Be aware that our greatest rewards will not be found in this life but in the next. Jesus warned us not to store up treasures on earth that can be lost and destroyed but store up treasures in heaven. For where our treasures are, there our hearts will be also (Matthew 6:19-20).

While difficult to achieve, the ordinances of the Lord are proclaimed for our own good and are "more to be desired than gold, even much fine gold, sweeter also than honey and the drippings of the honeycomb" (Psalm 19:10).

Let us learn what par is for our lives, do our best to achieve it and finish the course with honor.

Jesus replied, " 'You must love the Lord your God with all your heart, all your soul, and all your mind.' This is the first and greatest commandment. A second is equally important: 'Love your neighbor as yourself.' All the other commandments and all the demands of the prophets are based on these two commandments."

Matthew 22:37-40

Shooting Par

Completing one hole of golf reminds me of living one day. Each stands on its own but is linked to the next. Before I begin a hole, I have an idea about what lies ahead. I drive the ball, either down the fairway or into the rough. No matter, I must take the next shot. Days are like that. I have a plan for the day. The first task or adventure may go smoothly as planned or I may be thrown off course. Whatever happens, I must continue and move forward.

Beginning at the first hole, my plan is to shoot par. Whenever I get off course or in the rough, I attempt to return to the fairway and strive to finish the hole shooting as close to par as possible. It is the same with my daily life. I know God's commands and what God expects from me but I do not always do what I should do. Then, I need to get back on course striving to achieve God's will.

My challenge in shooting par in life is that, once aware of God's guidance, I don't do what I should. I am self-centered, trying to do my will, to get ahead on my own and to accomplish my agenda. Instead, I should focus on discovering God's will and putting His will ahead of my own.

Just as we need to learn the rules of golf to compete and win the match, we need to learn God's rules to live as God desires us to live. How do we do that? We study his Holy Word, the Bible, and meditate upon it. To be knowledgeable on the course, a golfer must devote time to reading and learning the rules. Christians must devote time to study, pray about, and meditate on the Scriptures to learn and follow God's will.

As the Lord advised Joshua, "This book of the law shall not depart out of your mouth; you shall meditate on it day and night, so that you may be careful to act in accordance with all that is written in it. For then you shall make your way prosperous, and then you shall be successful" (Joshua 1:8).

It's hard and challenging, but let's strive to reach God's par each day.

For I do not do the good I want, but the evil I do not want is what I do. Now if I do what I do not want, it is no longer I that do it, but sin that dwells within me. So I find it to be a law that when I want to do what is good, evil lies close at hand. Romans 7: 19-20

Keep Score – Stroke Play

Keeping score in golf is easy because scores are entered on the scorecard at the conclusion of each hole. We don't record our own scores, but keep our opponents' scores, and they keep ours. At the end of the round, each scorer signs his or her name to the card and gives it to the other player. After players have checked the scores, they sign their cards and the scores are official.

Each player should carefully check the card because the player is accountable for the accuracy of the score recorded for each hole under his or her name – the opponent isn't. The player is responsible for any mistakes which can't be changed later, even on the testimony of witnesses.

In stroke play, each stroke played is counted and totaled by hole. Penalty strokes, as required, may be added. At the conclusion of the round, the player with the lowest number of stroke wins.

In the game of life, think of strokes as sins. Just as in golf, we want to keep our strokes low. We stroke each time we sin or come up short of God's mark. As we keep our scorecard, we must not become lax or fail to count every sin. We might be tempted to only count the obvious sins of commission or maybe only the big ones and overlook the sins of omission.

Our attempt at scorekeeping is futile. None of our own scoring matters as God is really keeping the record. His scorecard is official. There is no fudging, no chance of error and no time for correction. "For he will repay according to each one's deeds: to those who by patiently doing good seek for glory and honor and immortality, he will give eternal life; while for those who are self-seeking and who obey not the truth but wickedness, there will be wrath and fury" (Romans 2:6-8).

The consequences of judgment come in close proximity to death. We are told, "Just as it is appointed for mortals to die once, and after that the judgment" (Hebrews 9:27). There will come a day of accounting and judgment before Jesus. We each have rebelled against God; so, we should repent and prepare for our day to meet Jesus who died for our sins. We can let Jesus' scorecard be seen in place of ours and live lives worthy of receiving His honor.

For all of us must appear before the judgment seat of Christ, so that each may receive recompense for what has been done in the body, whether good or evil. 2 Corinthians 5:10

Keep Score – Match Play

Scoring for stroke play and match play is slightly different. In stroke play, each stroke taken is counted and totaled by hole. As required, penalty strokes may be added. In match play, the score is recorded as holes up or holes down. The player with the lowest score per hole wins or is "one up" for that hole. We don't need to write down our actual score; we simply count the number of holes we've won or lost. The player with the most holes up wins.

In the game of life, we can try to keep our score – how well we are living in accordance with God's rules. We generally know when we are following God's commands and when we sin. We may believe that we are doing pretty well, at least compared to others. It is a very human tendency to measure our performance against that we observe in others.

Perhaps, most of us prefer to be scored as match play versus others instead of stroke play. We like to believe that we are better than _____. (You fill in the blank.)

In a recent survey, respondents expressed the belief that not all persons will go to heaven but that they, their families and their friends will be there. It seems fine when we do our own scorekeeping. We like comparisons that we make, but we are at a disadvantage when each stroke or sin is counted against us.

In life we are judged by God and, while we may prefer to be graded on the curve against the performance of others, that is not God's system. We are not in a match against others but are on our own. We are to live a life pleasing to God as we strive to achieve God's standards.

None of our own scorekeeping matters as God is keeping the record. His record is official. There is no fudging on his scorecard, no chance of error and no time for correction. "I tell you, on the day of judgment you will have to give an account for every careless word you utter; for by your words you will be justified, and by your words you will be condemned" (Matthew 12:36-37). There will come a day of accounting and judgment before Him. Like a Boy Scout, be prepared!

He commanded us to preach to the people and to testify that he is the one ordained by God as judge of the living and the dead. Acts 10:42

Establishing a Handicap

To make the game competitive for golfers of all ability levels, the United States Golf Association administers a handicapping system, referred to as the "average best" method, which was introduced in the early 20th Century. A handicap is calculated using a specific arithmetic formula approximating how many strokes above or below par a player should be expected to play. A USGA Handicap Index can be established with as few as five scores. As additional scores are posted, the handicap will be figured using the lowest 10 of the most recent 20 rounds.

A player's handicap is intended to show potential, not a player's average score. How often a golfer will play to his or her handicap is a function of that person's handicap, as low handicappers are statistically more consistent than higher handicappers. In handicapped competition, the golfer who shoots the best with respect to his documented abilities should win. A golfer's net score is determined by subtracting the player's handicap from the gross score (the number of strokes actually taken). The net scores of all the competing golfers are compared and the person with the lowest score wins.

All people have handicaps in that we are not gifted with the same physical and mental abilities and skills. Individual Christians do not have the same spiritual gifts or capabilities, but we each have help to discover our gifts. "Now we have received not the spirit of the world, but the Spirit that is from God, so that we may understand the gifts bestowed on us by God" (1 Corinthians 2:12).

Every person is valuable to the body of Christ and adds to the function of the body. We should each strive to discover our gifts and talents and put them to work for the Kingdom of God.

Just as the human body cannot function optimally without all its parts, the Body of Christ cannot be at its best without every one of its members functioning with the gifts that each has been given. Let's discover our talents and spiritual gifts and put them to work for the Lord. Then, we can play to our full potential whether we are scratch, bogie or novice golfers.

We have gifts that differ according to the grace given to us: prophecy, in proportion to faith; ministry, in ministering; the teacher, in teaching; the exhorter, in exhortation; the giver, in generosity; the leader, in diligence; the compassionate, in cheerfulness. Romans 12:6-8

The Golfer

Lesson Book

When I took lessons at a three-day Golf Digest Instructional School, the instructors provided a workbook divided into sections on full swing, putting, short approaches, sand play and practice/strategy. The notebook included some common instruction, but mostly provided pages of forms to be completed by the student based on individual instruction.

Each page was structured to denote the area of instruction with lines to enter the swing corrections given, the reasons for the corrections, practice drills to improve performance, and the feel of the correction. The instructors emphasized that the students should use their workbooks after completing the school in order to reinforce learning and improve their golf games. They emphasized that exposure to instruction without practice will not lead to improvement. In order to master the game, it is necessary to return to the book of instructions repeatedly.

So it is with living life to the fullest as God would have us live. He has provided in the Bible the best and most appropriate guidance for life. For Joshua and the Israelites,

God made available the Book of the Law (the Pentateuch). He instructed Joshua and all the people to learn and meditate on it – to inculcate it into their very being.

Paul instructed his protégé Timothy regarding the use of the sacred writings. "All Scripture is inspired by God and is useful for teaching, for reproof, for correction, and for training in righteousness, so that everyone who belongs to God may be proficient, equipped for every good work" (2 Timothy 3:16-17).

Just as I need to reread and learn the material in my golf instruction workbook to master the game of golf, we each should study and meditate on the Word of God, the Bible, to master the serious living of life. The more we do so; the more we internalize God's messages. "I delight to do Your will, O my God; Your Law is within my heart" (Psalm 40:8). Let's each commit to instill the Word of God into our very being so that we may experience the successful and flourishing lives God desires for us.

This book of the law shall not depart from your mouth, but you shall meditate on it day and night, so that you may be careful to do according to all that is written in it; for then you will make your way prosperous, and then you will have success. Joshua 1:8

Training and Practice

I like to play the game of golf, get out on the course and take the shots. I like to walk the fairways and enjoy the camaraderie of other golfers. But, practice is a different story; it can be laborious or boring. Nonetheless, whether one is a beginner, a well-seasoned amateur or even a professional golfer, if we are not happy with our game or just want to progress, practice is necessary.

Practice is not just standing in place and swinging a club. We must be focused and strive for improvement. When we are working to develop a specific element of our swing or our putts, we must work correctly on our technique, even if we miss the ball or the hole, until we don't miss them anymore. We can practice techniques and we can employ golf training aids to help with many aspects of our game.

To enhance performance, we can use practice drills to maintain our posture, become accurate in repeating a stroke, accelerate at the right time to square up the face at impact, and refine the plane of the swing. Practice drills help to focus on whatever it is that we are trying mechanically to improve. When it's time to play, however, forget mechanics and concentrate on the target. Learn to separate playing from practice.

Likewise, if we want to live a life in accordance with God's laws and ordnances, we must also practice. That means doing the right things not only when others are present and watching but, also, when we are alone. That is when we are practicing. It may seem easy for us to get away with something when no one knows what we are doing, but that is the time to practice doing the right thing. Apply the old adage, practice makes perfect; be diligent and don't be lazy.

We can set a life goal to strive for the perfection demonstrated for us by Jesus. Even when he was alone in the wilderness being tempted by the devil, Jesus resisted all temptations, thwarting them by reliance on the Word of God. Then the devil left him and, suddenly, angels came and waited on him (Matthew 4:11). God gave us the model, provides us with the training aids and gives us the strength to achieve his will. We should practice by doing the right things when we are alone.

The appetite of the lazy craves, and gets nothing, while the appetite of the diligent is richly supplied. Proverbs 13:4

Different Golfers – Different Skills

Golfers arrive at the course with different levels of ability and skill. A new golfer has little instruction covering the basic shots, has minimal on-course playing experience and is not familiar with the rules and etiquette of golf. An advanced beginner has some playing experience and increasing ability to execute shots. An intermediate player plays regularly, knows and plays by the rules, and has an established handicap.

A skillful player may play a couple times a week and have a handicap below 20. An advanced player plays frequently and is comfortable in match and tournament play. Roger Gunn, a Californian who teaches golf professionals, has categorized golfers into five levels: beginners, 30-20 handicappers, 19-12 handicappers, 11-5 handicappers and 4-scratch golfers.

Golf is one sport that allows players of different calibers to play equitably and competitively against each other by using the handicap system. By establishing handicaps, all golfers can compete fairly and enjoy playing with each other. Golf can even be played as a team sport as in college competition.

Paul described the church functioning effectively together as a body. Through the Spirit, all Christians are baptized into one body and, just as the human body is comprised of numerous seen and unseen parts, so, the church is comprised of many diverse members. Clergy and lay leaders are highly visible while administrative and kitchen workers may be hidden from view. All are essential and each impacts the other. When one suffers, all suffer and when one receives honor, all rejoice together.

God provides each member with different talents and abilities and each Christian, no matter his or her level of skill, contributes to the body of the church. Every member, weak or strong, is important and, unlike playing golf, when all come together without competition, the church prospers. "God has so arranged the body, giving the greater honor to the inferior member, that there may be no dissension within the body, but the members may have the same care for one another" (1Corinthians 12:24b-25). We are blessed to become messengers of Jesus and to spread that blessing to others.

If the whole body were an eye, where would the hearing be? If the whole body were hearing, where would the sense of smell be? But as it is, God arranged the members in the body, each one of them, as he chose. 1 Corinthians 12:17-18

Betting

Although not addressed in the USGA's *The Rules of Golf*, golf and gambling go hand-in-glove for many golfers. Wagers may be large or small and bets as varied as you can imagine.

The Nassau is three bets in one: low score on the front nine, low score on the back nine and low score over the full 18. The $2 Nassau is perhaps the most common bet on the course. Round Robin, also known as Hollywood or Sixes, is a betting game that involves two members of the foursome teaming up against the other two. The partners rotate every six holes.

In Wolf players rotate as the "Wolf." On each hole, the player designated as the Wolf has to choose whether to play 1 against 3, or 2 on 2 with the Wolf choosing a partner. The Wolf can win or lose more money by playing alone.

Sandies may be side bets. A golfer automatically wins the bet either by making par on a hole in which he was in a sand trap or by getting up-and-down from a greenside bunker. Bingo Bango Bongo awards points throughout the round for three different pre-designated accomplishments, such as first on the green. At the end of the round, points are totaled and the differences are paid.

Barkies, sometimes called Woodies or Seves (as in Seve Ballesteros), are earned by any player who makes par on a hole after having hit a tree. Arnies (as in Arnold Palmer) are won by any golfer who makes a par without having managed to hit his ball into the fairway.

Betting can be complicated and keeping up with all the side bets may get confusing. Dishonesty in reporting results may present an opportunity and may appear to pay off short-term, but will lead to future slips and falls. Author Spencer Johnson said, "Integrity is telling myself the truth. And honesty is telling the truth to other people." Our challenge is to both have integrity and be honest.

As in any endeavor, the golfer, ultimately, profits most for himself and in his relationships with others by declaring an honest score. Golfers must be on firm footing to play their best; likewise, demonstrating integrity in reporting results will pay many future dividends. I'll bet you knew that!

People with integrity have firm footing, but those who follow crooked paths will slip and fall. Proverbs 10:9

Size Doesn't Matter

Golfers come in all sizes. Perhaps the shortest male to have played as a professional is Ian Woosnam at 5' 4" and the tallest is Phil Blackmar at 6' 8". Champion golfers come in all heights, for example: Ben Hogan and Chi Chi Rodriguez at 5' 7"; Bobby Jones at 5' 8"; Tom Kite, Tom Watson and Rory McIlroy at 5' 9"; Arnold Palmer and Jack Nicklaus at 5' 10"; Sam Snead at 5' 11"; Tiger Woods at 6' 0"; Vijay Singh at 6' 2" and Phil Mickelson at 6' 3".

Theoretically, a lower center of gravity would advantage shorter players when playing in substantial wind or on uneven ground. On the other hand, taller players can produce a wider swing arc and, therefore, should have the advantage in gaining more distance and creating a higher trajectory when necessary. While each theoretical advantage assumes that all other things are equal, that is never the case. Size alone is no determiner of success in golf. Knowledge, practice, skill, physical conditioning, focus and motivation are all components of championship golfers.

Zacchaeus was a short man who was determined to see Jesus, but a crowd had gathered as Jesus entered Jericho. Since Zacchaeus could not see over the crowd, he used his mental ability and decided to run ahead and climb a sycamore tree in order to see. This action produced an unexpected result as Jesus spotted Zacchaeus and asked to stay at his house. Zacchaeus sought and accepted Jesus who declared that salvation had come to the house of Zacchaeus that day.

Luke tells us that Jesus said he came to seek and save the lost (19:10). Their height or any other physical characteristic did not matter to him. We are all lost sinners in need of Jesus' salvation and are all welcomed into the Kingdom of God when we repent and acknowledge him as our Savior and Lord. Regardless of our size or any other physical characteristics, when we accept Jesus' sacrifice for our sins, each of us becomes an eternal winner. Zacchaeus sought out Jesus. If you have not, do it today.

A man was there named Zacchaeus; he was a chief tax-collector and was rich. He was trying to see who Jesus was, but on account of the crowd he could not, because he was short in stature. Luke 19:2-3

The Course

Golf Course Design

Members of the American Society of Golf Course Architects, founded in 1946, have designed, renovated and remodeled many of golf's most famous courses. The finest design enhances the natural beauty of the course's location while using the terrain to create challenging and enjoyable golf experiences. Earlier architects who designed the Pine Valley Golf Course in 1918 and the Pebble Beach Golf Links in 1919 demonstrated how land could be shaped into beautiful and challenging courses.

A well-designed course has a mixture of diverse holes which provide reasonable challenges for average golfers. Some have straight fairways and others have doglegs or sharp turns that are more difficult to play. The green, the goal for the golfer and the nightmare of groundskeepers, should be designed to make putting challenging without being overly difficult. Each degree of slope and grass height makes a difference in the game. The finest design of hazards (creeks, ponds, bunkers, and places with plants and trees) incorporates visual appeal while challenging the players. The roughs featuring lush vegetation, tall trees and long grass definitely impact the golfer's game.

Most golf course architecture is geared toward design that challenges professionals while still keeping the course playable by amateurs, abiding by Robert Trent Jones Sr.'s maxim that a hole should be "a hard par but an easy bogey."

The beginning design of each hole is dictated by the natural terrain of the course which means that God is the ultimate course designer. After all, in the beginning God created the heavens and the earth. Then God said, "Let us make humankind in our image, according to our likeness" (Genesis 1:26a).

We are blessed to be made in the image of God and be able to play on the ground and over the terrain that God created. The game of life is challenging to all of us but God designed our course of life to be playable by amateurs (all of us). We can play it best as we partner with and worship God, the Creator.

God saw everything that he had made, and indeed, it was very good. And there was evening and there was morning, the sixth day.
Genesis 1:31

Maintenance Workers

I like to play golf in the morning when the sun has just risen, the air is clear and there is no one in front. With the first tee time, my friends and I can move at a steady pace without excessive waiting. It seems like we have our own private course.

Yet, there is one drawback with early morning golf. This is the time when most maintenance workers are likely to be on the course. They cut the grass, groom the bunkers, blow the leaves, fertilize the greens, clean up after storms and perform other odd jobs to prepare the course. They are a necessary and vital part of the game of golf.

It is easy to become annoyed with the sound of the mowers and other power equipment. Early morning golfers play in an atmosphere to which professionals would not be exposed or tolerate. Once, Tiger Woods was annoyed by a camera shutter clicking while he was preparing to putt. Imagine what would happen if the mowing tractor came by.

Maintenance workers do jobs many others would not do. They work for minimal pay in all kinds of weather while watching others enjoy a leisure pastime they may envy. They may easily perceive an inequity in that. When I pass workers on the course, I try to remember to treat them with the dignity that we each inherit as we are all created in God's image. He loves each one of us. We can do little things like acknowledging the person's presence, saying "Good morning," and thanking them for stopping their work while we play through.

We should treat these people who are least on the golf course as if we were encountering Jesus for He said that in doing so we would be doing it to Him. Maintenance workers are vitally important to the game of golf for there would be no playable courses without them.

We are all, from the least to the greatest, important to the Son of God for He created, sustains and redeems us. The maintenance worker is just as much our neighbor as a professional golfer or our favorite golf buddy. When we recognize and respond with love and respect to all, we find that we are not only successful players on the golf course, but also in the kingdom of God.

Then he will answer them, "Truly I tell you, just as you did not do it to one of the least of these, you did not do it to me." Matthew 25:45

Caddies

In golf, a caddie carries a player's bag and clubs, and gives insightful advice, encouragement and moral support. Competent caddies are aware of the challenges and obstacles of the golf course being played. They recognize the best strategies for playing it by knowing overall yardage, terrain, pin placements and club selection. Traditionally, the golfer and the caddie walk the course with the caddie out in front of the player.

For players riding carts, a fore-caddie will give a description of the hole to the players and walk ahead to spot the landings of the tee shots. The fore-caddie then determines the players' yardage (either with a laser, course knowledge, or yardage-marked sprinkler heads) for their next shots. This process continues until the players reach the green.

Once on the green the caddie may read greens, clean golf balls, fix ball marks, and tend the flag. The caddie is responsible for raking sand traps on the course. More than anything else, the caddy is a helper to make the player's round enjoyable by taking care of ancillary tasks, speeding up play, and providing course knowledge and motivational support.

When Jesus knew the time for his crucifixion was near, he told his disciples that he would leave them. He was returning to the Father and at that time they could not come with him, but he promised not to leave them on their own. He said he would send the Helper to them. The disciples did not understand. Jesus explained, "Nevertheless, I tell you the truth: it is to your advantage that I go away, for if I do not go away, the Advocate (Helper) will not come to you; but if I go, I will send him to you" (John 16:7). The Helper will testify on Jesus' behalf, teach the disciples, and remind them of all that Jesus said to them.

The Advocate or Holy Spirit was sent by Jesus to be the Helper to each Christian – to support, encourage, enlighten, and illumine Jesus' followers. The Holy Spirit guides us to avoid spiritual dangers and to overcome temptations. The Spirit of God to a Christian is somewhat like a caddie to a golfer – by his side, knowing all the rules, techniques and lay of the land to guide and point the way through our earthly journey. Unlike a paid caddie, however, the Holy Spirit comes as a free gift when we accept Jesus as our Savior. Thank God for the Spirit.

And I will ask the Father, and he will give you another Advocate (Helper), to be with you for ever. John 14.16

The Undulated Green

To be undulated means to have a wavy surface. Why should course designers make putting easy by providing smooth, flat surfaces on the greens? Why not create little hills and valleys? Why not make the golfer putt across the slope of a hill or up the hill and through the valley? Such challenges must delight golf course designers. The answers come in the form of challenging greens that are anything but flat.

Undulated greens challenge golfers to read the greens to find the right path to the holes. Golfers must take into account the slope and tilt of the ground, moisture on the green, the length of the grass and the direction of the grass grain. Even with the best read, the result is not guaranteed. Peter Jacobson, winner of seven PGA tour events, once said, "I didn't miss the putt. I made the putt. The ball missed the hole."

Greg Norman designed the TPC San Antonio AT&T Oaks Course that opened in February 2010. It is described as having "huge undulated greens with shaved banks that create a lot of problems for players who come up short or long, or simply miss the putting surface on either side of the glass-like greens." The design of the greens was part of keeping the terrain natural.

There are plenty of ups and downs in the natural world. We seldom have a smooth, straight path as we travel the road of life but must learn to "read the terrain" to move appropriately toward the goal of eternal life with our Lord. While the path we follow crosses hills and valleys, God has promised to provide guidance which we find throughout the Bible. We are reminded by the psalmists, "The Lord exists forever; your word is firmly fixed in the heaven. Your faithfulness endures to all generations" (Psalm 119:89-90a). "Your word is a lamp to my feet and a light to my path" (Psalm 119:105).

Life is hard, but Jesus promised to be with us always on our journey. "And remember, I am with you always, to the end of the age" (Matthew 28:20b). When, in faith, we accept Jesus as our Lord and become his disciples, we still need to read the lay of the land. We have his Word to guide us over the hilly terrain of life and his promise to be with us as we strive towards our final goal.

Lord, you show me the path of life. In your presence there is fullness of joy; in your right hand are pleasures for evermore. Psalm 16:11

Wind

We cannot see it; yet, we know it is there. We feel it and observe its effects in the flutter of leaves or swaying of trees. It may be very faint and gentle in the summer. In the spring, on the coast, on top of a mountain or in a storm, it may be fierce and strong. The presence of the wind is one determining factor in the flight of a golf ball.

Under the *The Rules of Golf*, a golf ball may weigh no more than 1.62 ounces, have a diameter not less than 1.68 inches, and not exceed a maximum velocity of 250 feet per second under test conditions. Moving through the air, an object this small and light is subject to the vicissitudes of steady, shifting or swirling wind. Any spin on the ball exacerbates the wind's influence.

Professional golfers often toss grass into the air to ascertain the effect of wind. They visualize the direction (front, behind or across) and the velocity to determine if they need to use a club for more or less distance than the measured length of the shot and whether to aim to the right or left of the target. While the wind is not seen, it is felt and affects on the golf shot.

The Spirit of God is like the wind – present but unseen. Once, Jesus was approached by the Pharisee Nicodemis who recognized that Jesus was filled with the presence of God. Jesus told Nicodemis that his followers must be spirit-filled by saying, "Very truly, I tell you, no one can enter the kingdom of God without being born of water and Spirit. What is born of the flesh is flesh, and what is born of the Spirit is spirit. Do not be astonished that I said to you, 'You must be born from above'" (John 3:5-7). Jesus said He came from the Father into the world and was returning to the Father; but, He was sending the Spirit of truth to testify on His behalf. The Spirit will illuminate sin, righteousness and judgment.

The Spirit is unseen and omnipresent, sometimes as a gentle breeze and other times as a mighty gale, but always guiding us into all the truth. We should become as aware of the influence of the Spirit on our lives as we are of the influence of the wind on the golf ball. In life as in golf, taking advantage of the wind (Holy Spirit), instead of ignoring it, results in our best shots.

The wind blows where it chooses, and you hear the sound of it, but you do not know where it comes from or where it goes. So it is with everyone who is born of the Spirit. John 3:8

Reflection

Gazing out at the par 3 hole, I stood on the elevated tee overlooking the water in front of the green. The azaleas were blooming and the lime-green leaves had burst out on the surrounding trees. The images of spring were reflected in the pond below.

There, shimmering on the top of the lake were the images of flowering nature. It was not the real plants and trees, but a reasonable facsimile. All the forms were visible but many details were missing. On the water were reflected clear, precise, remarkable reproductions – not the real things but pleasurable in their own right.

I teed up the ball, hit it and high it flew. To my dismay, it landed in the pond, creating concentric ripples when it entered the water. The images became distorted. Of course, it did not have to be the golf ball that disturbed the water. It could have been merely the wind causing waves to lap the shore or rain beating down on the water's surface. With the slightest disruption the images became altered. With enough disturbances, the images would become completely altered, unclear and unrecognizable.

Males and females are created in the image of God, as reflections of God, not the real thing. Some components and characteristics are missing. They were clearer images when Adam and Eve were created in the Garden. "God saw everything that he had made, and indeed, it was very good" (Genesis 1:31). Once sin entered the picture, the images became more distorted. Excessive sin and rebellion can even lead to the point of losing most of the image of God altogether.

God said, "Let us create man in our image, according to our likeness" (Genesis 1:26a). What parts of "our image" did God mean? Certainly, God did not mean omniscience, omnipotence or omnipresence. In wisdom, God did not create mankind with these three attributes. Can you imagine creating and turning loose so many little gods to run free?

Maybe we were created mostly in the image of love. When we love God, neighbor, enemy and self, God's image becomes clear. The waves on the water subside to ripples and, in our best times, are even smooth.

So God created humankind in his image, in the image of God he created them; male and female he created them. God blessed them.
Genesis 1:27-28a

Rain

I have an unspoken rule – never play golf in the rain. Well, sometimes I do, but it is usually unintentional. When I do, the rule becomes spoken out loud, "I will never play in the rain again!" Then, there are times when a shower occurs unexpectedly and times when a tournament or planned event must be played in inclement weather. Whether I like it or not, the rain arrives and I must meet the challenge and prevail through the drizzle or downpour.

Rain makes golfers uncomfortable and, sometimes, unpleasant. Proper dress for protection against the rain is critical, as a soaked, wet golfer cannot focus on the game or play well. Protection is provided with an umbrella, a proper rain suit, a supply of dry gloves or rain gloves and towels.

A primary imperative for playing in the rain is to keep the club grips and hands dry. Without solid hand contact on the grips, a player will not strike the ball accurately. Even worse, the club may fly out of the hands in the middle of the swing, something dangerous to anyone nearby.

Just as unexpected rain assaults golfers and tests our skills, preparation, and fortitude; so, the forces of evil will assault Christians. They, like golfers, must be equipped ahead of time to repel every attack. "Therefore take up the whole armor of God, so that you may be able to withstand on that evil day, and having done everything, to stand firm" (Ephesians 6:13). To be victorious in this battle, Christians must be prepared.

Wear the armor of the Lord: the belt of truth, the breastplate of righteousness, the shield of faith, the helmet of salvation, and the sword of the Spirit, which is the Word of God. Be ready and willing to proclaim the gospel of peace. With these protections that the Lord provides, we can withstand the storms of life and the wiles of the devil. Keep alert, pray and persevere. At the end of the storms we will find the One who in his everlasting love has been with us in our travail – Jesus, the Light of the world.

Finally, be strong in the Lord and in the strength of his power. Put on the whole armor of God, so that you may be able to stand against the wiles of the devil. Ephesians 6:10-11

Fire

A person can use a golf club for many non-golf purposes – hiking stick, fishing rod or weapon. But, on August 31, 2010 a golf club was put to a different use. During a golfer's routine swing in the rough at the Shady Canyon Golf Course in Irvine, CA, his club struck a rock. This sounds like something that could happen to any one of us. Only on this windy day, the impact caused a spark which set off a blaze that eventually burned 25 acres and required the efforts of 150 Orange County firefighters to extinguish.

Forget "Fore!" The cry of the day for that golfer was "Fire!" Officials say the fire burned through the rough into vegetation next to the course and, then, over two dry, brushy hillsides. No charges were filed against the golfer, whose name was withheld.

Fire can begin quickly and move fast, particularly when impelled by the wind. On the day of Pentecost, the followers of the risen Jesus were gathered together at one place in Jerusalem. Suddenly, there came a sound like the rush of a violent wind as tongues like fire appeared. The wind was perhaps the same as that in the creation story in Genesis 1:2b where "a wind from God swept over the face of the waters."

At Pentecost, the wind was the coming of the Holy Spirit, which moved rapidly, like fire, and enabled the followers of Jesus to communicate with each other. Devout people, gathered from many parts of the known world, were speaking their own languages and understood each other in their own language. They were told, "Everyone who calls on the name of the Lord shall be saved" (Acts 2:21). How was that to happen? "Peter said to them, 'Repent, and be baptized every one of you in the name of Jesus Christ so that your sins may be forgiven; and you will receive the gift of the Holy Spirit'" (Acts 2:38).

We do not know where the spark of the Holy Spirit will ignite the flame of faith. But, we know it can happen at any time in any place. We can and should be prepared to share our faith and rely on the power and grace of the Holy Spirit to ignite that faith in others.

Divided tongues, as of fire, appeared among them, and a tongue rested on each of them. Acts 2:3

Clouds

One bright, crisp Wednesday morning in early October, I stood on the 6th tee. The sun was shining and the sky was Carolina blue. On this perfect morning for golf, I looked down the hill toward the creek and up the next rise to the elevated green. After driving the ball, I noticed overhead widely-disbursed, billowing, cumulus clouds – fluffy and alluring. There are lots of other clouds, including the dark, ominous rain clouds that are not welcome on the golf course. But, on this day those clouds were captivating.

I thought about Jesus' words in Matthew 26:64 as he confirmed his role as Messiah, the Son of God. The clouds I saw that morning would be the perfect clouds for Jesus' second coming in power and glory.

Clouds have been associated with God since the days of the Israelites' exodus from Egypt. "The Lord went in front of them in a pillar of cloud by day, to lead them along the way, and in a pillar of fire by night, to give them light, so that they might travel by day and by night" (Exodus 13:21). The Lord told Moses, "I am going to come to you in a dense cloud, in order that the people may hear when I speak with you and so trust you ever after" (Exodus 19.9b).

In the 6th century BCE in Babylon, the prophet Ezekiel described his encounter with the Lord, "Like the bow in a cloud on a rainy day, such was the appearance of the splendor all round. This was the appearance of the likeness of the glory of the Lord. When I saw it, I fell on my face, and I heard the voice of someone speaking" (Ezekiel 1.28).

Such images from the Hebrew Scriptures must have come to mind to his disciples when Jesus ascended to heaven. He told them that no one but the Father knows when he will restore the kingdom of Israel. "When he had said this, as they were watching, he was lifted up, and a cloud took him out of their sight" (Acts 1:9). Two men in white robes told them, "This Jesus, who has been taken up from you into heaven, will come in the same way as you saw him go into heaven" (Acts 1:11b).

On that October morning on the golf course, I thought – it will be on one of these kinds of clouds that Jesus will come again. Praise God!

From now on you will see the Son of Man seated at the right hand of Power and coming on the clouds of heaven. Matthew 26:64b

The Play

Plan Strategy

Bobby Jones said, "Golf is a game played on a five-inch course – the distance between your ears." He meant the golfer must think about the game both before and during play. Successful golfers will develop and implement a strategy for each round that is more than just planning to hit the ball into a certain position for the next shot. They will think about the game ahead of time while, also, making adjustments along the way.

Ben Hogan often would walk a course the evening before a tournament to observe and learn its subtleties and, what he called, its "tricks and traps." This was how he mentally prepared, strategized and focused on the golf round.

Some rounds need more preparation than others. Navatanee Golf Course, built to host the 23rd World Cup of Golf in 1975, advertises "a golf course that every golfer playing in Thailand needs to try at least once. This is a course that demands planning and strategy from the tee to the green and golfers should be warned to bring lots of extra balls." Wherever we play, planning a golf strategy is important.

The same advice is applicable to our lives as Christians. Peter tells us in his Second Letter that a day of judgment is coming and that the Lord does not want any to perish but all to come to repentance. Nonetheless, there will be destruction of the godless (2 Peter 3:7). On that day the heavens and the earth will pass away and be replaced with new heavens and a new earth. Like the golfer facing a challenging course, we are to plan for this and implement a strategy to accept Jesus and in gratitude live blamelessly in order to take advantage of the opportunity God gives us to repent.

Life is filled with temptations to veer off course but the Lord is patient with us. We should avail ourselves of His grace and live righteous lives guided by a plan and strategy to follow the ordinances of the Lord and to adjust our behavior as we daily stray from His Holy plan. Commit, today, to grow in the knowledge and grace of our Lord and Savior Jesus Christ.

But, in accordance with his promise, we wait for new heavens and a new earth, where righteousness is at home. Therefore, beloved, while you are waiting for these things, strive to be found by him at peace, without spot or blemish; and regard the patience of our Lord as salvation. 2 Peter 3:13-15a

Align Shots

Greg Norman said, "Of all the things you do before you play a golf shot, setting your alignment is the most important. And certainly, it requires the closest attention." He noted that on a tee-shot, a five degree error in alignment can usually mean a ball in the rough rather than the fairway. A 10 degree error may mean a hazard, a lost ball, or out-of-bounds. Proper alignment is critical all the way to and on the green.

For proper alignment, position yourself about 10 feet directly behind the ball, keeping the ball between yourself and the target. Pick a spot on the ground about 3 feet in front of the ball that is on the line to the target. Move to the side of the ball and take your stance parallel to your target line. Address the ball, keeping your body square to the target line with your toes, knees, hips, and shoulders parallel to your target line. Position the club behind the ball with the clubface pointed squarely towards the target spot in front of the ball. Now you are ready to swing your club.

Wise men from the East came to Bethlehem to pay homage to Jesus after his birth. These were well-educated, political officials in the courts of Parthia (now northeastern Iran), Armenia or other regions east of Judea, who were adhering to their tradition of honoring and giving gifts to new rulers or kings. They followed the guiding star seeking the new king of Israel prophesied by Micah 700 years before Jesus' birth. They chose their objective, aligned themselves with the star and proceed on their journey. After offering Jesus gifts of gold, frankincense and myrrh, they returned to their own countries.

Jesus is the King of kings, the sovereign who guides, sustains and protects us every day. We, Jesus' creation, are subjects, servants of the King, who told us how to align ourselves with Him. "If any want to become my followers, let them deny themselves and take up their cross and follow me" (Matthew 16:24b). Let us put Jesus' will ahead of our own and follow his perfect alignment to live today in the Kingdom of God.

There, ahead of them, went the star that they had seen at its rising, until it stopped over the place where the child was.
Matthew 2:9b

Be Positive

Golf is not about hitting the ball; it's about where you hit the ball – about the target. It involves focus. Here, thoughts are critical. Have you ever noticed that when you think about what you don't want, you get it? Don't fall for that. Focus on the positive – on where you want the ball to go.

Be aware of your thoughts – listen to yourself. If you do not see what you want or if it does not feel right, stop. Have the discipline and patience to back away and start again. Focus, on what you want, rather than on what you don't want.

Sometimes golfers think: *I don't want to slice this ball* or *I don't want to raise up during this shot*. Such thoughts can become self-fulfilling prophesy. Only think positively about what you want to happen and congratulate yourself for your wins. Think: *I am going to hit this ball down the middle.*

Designers of golf course are crafty and sometimes design holes to create optical illusions in an effort to attract the golfer's focus on the hazards and boundaries. Don't follow that visual lure to focus on the hazards; instead, concentrate on where you want to hit the ball and go for it!

In our work, our relationships and our everyday living, we can encounter real or perceived hazards and obstacles. We can become fearful of something going wrong or see the opportunity for failure staring us in the face. We should learn from golf to focus on the positive outcome that we most desire. Focusing on the negative is merely a destructive form of worry.

Jesus told his disciples to forget worrying. God values the birds and supplies feed for them, but He values humans even more and provides for our care. Jesus asked, "Can any of you by worrying, add a single hour to your span of life?" (Matthew 6:27). The Father knows what we need to sustain us and Jesus said, "Strive for the kingdom of God and these things will be given to you as well" (Matthew 6:33). As Christians, we are to strive toward the positive – living life following the precepts and commands of God. If we focus on the positive, on accomplishing His will for us, and dismiss from our thoughts the things we should avoid, we will complete our course with honor.

He said to his disciples, 'Therefore I tell you, do not worry about your life, what you will eat, or about your body, what you will wear. Luke 12:22

Avoid Danger

Golf can be enjoyed even when played in unfavorable weather conditions. In the cold, we can suit up in clothing layers; in hot weather we can wear shorts. However, there is nothing enjoyable about playing with lightning in the vicinity. It was said of Sam Snead. "He is only afraid of three things: Ben Hogan, downhill putts and lightning." Snead might not have admitted to the first two, but when storm clouds arrived, he headed for the clubhouse. So should we.

In 2010 the National Weather Service reported that typically 66 deaths from lightning occur every year with at least 3 of them happening on golf courses. The National Lightning Safety Institute reported that from 1990 to 2003 there were 756 lightning deaths in the United States. It advises operators of golf courses to install warning systems to alert golfers of lightning as close as six miles away. Most lightning injuries occur when people are not warned in time or fail to seek shelter. Upon hearing a weather siren, stop play.

As a storm approaches or signs of lightning appear ahead of a storm, seek shelter right away. Go back to the clubhouse, find a fully enclosed vehicle, a dense area of trees or bushes, or lie in a ditch. In the worse circumstances, if caught in an open area, become a small, low target.

When we are about to enter areas of danger in our lives, we receive warning signs. They may not be as loud as a weather siren, but we should be perceptive, heed their warnings and avoid the lurking dangers. Many of these dangers involve gratifying desires of the flesh, as Paul observed. "Now the works of the flesh are obvious: fornication, impurity, licentiousness, idolatry, sorcery, enmities, strife, jealousy, anger, quarrels, factions, envy, dissensions, drunkenness, carousing, and things like these. I am warning you, as I warned you before: those who do such things will not inherit the kingdom of God" (Galatians 5:19-21).

These temptations and actions, like lightning, usually provide advance warning of their approach but can strike quickly. We enter the paths of the wicked at our peril when we ignore the warning signs along the way. We should be aware of where we are headed and where we go. Be cautious around the works of the flesh and avoid danger.

Do not enter the path of the wicked, and do not walk in the way of evildoers. Avoid it; do not go on it; turn away from it and pass on. Proverbs 4:14-15

Keep It Simple

Every golfer should focus on the KISS – "Keep It Simple, Stupid!" Many of us make golf much more complicated than it needs to be. Beginning and average golfers spend time and energy thinking about everything. They digest multiple golf magazines that contain new tips each month, look at various videos that illustrate different techniques, watch "how to" shows on The Golf Channel, and focus on the pros on weekend TV. All this activity is directed towards seeking the magic to significantly improve their games.

This results in much diverse information and instruction competing in our heads. We think about changing our stance, rotating our grip, slowing the take away, modifying the backswing, turning the shoulders or hips to a certain angle and multiple other swing elements. Before we know it, we are perplexed as to what happened to our swing. Golf becomes way too complicated and seems like an impossible task.

On the course don't let the multiple, competing details get in the way of accomplishing the goal. Golfers often have to get back to the basics. Do the simple things like: aim accurately, keep your eyes on the ball, accelerate through the shot and hit down on the ball.

In a similar manner, Christians may think there are many steps and actions needed to be taken to be saved from their sins and be raised to eternal life with Jesus. What do the commandments really mean? How close can I come to violating what I believe the commandments say? How good do I have to be to get to heaven? Can I do enough good deeds to offset my sins? How can I know that I have been saved?

Don't get bogged down. Get back to the basics. God has a clear and concise plan of salvation and made it simple for us. We merely acknowledge that we are sinners, separated from God by our sins – our willful rebellion against God. Repent and turn away from sin and toward a life of pleasing God. Through faith, acknowledge the death and resurrection of Jesus Christ as the deliverance from our bondage to sin. Then, in trust and obedience to Christ as our Lord, enjoy a personal relationship with God for eternity. That's God's KISS – or kiss!

If you confess with your lips that Jesus is Lord and believe in your heart that God raised him from the dead, you will be saved.
Romans 10:9

Free Drop

Rule 28 of *The Rules of Golf* addresses an unplayable ball. During a match, a player may deem his ball unplayable at any place on the course, except when the ball is in a water hazard (addressed in rule 26).

The player is the sole judge as to whether his ball is unplayable. If the player considers his ball to be unplayable, he will incur a penalty of one stroke and must drop the ball one of the following ways: (1) where he originally hit the ball, (2) back on a line behind where the ball lies and the hole, or (3) two club lengths from the ball, no closer to the hole.

When the golfer has to drop a ball, he must stand up straight with the ball held at shoulder height and at an arm's length and drop it. It must not stop any closer to the hole than where the original ball was positioned. The player pays a penalty of one stroke but may continue play.

In life, we can easily despair when troubles in our job, troubles in our marriage or troubles in our relationships seem to overwhelm us. We may have physical problems or financial problems and feel that our life has become "unplayable." We may not know where to turn or how to move forward.

At such times when we feel defeated, we can relate to Paul, who said he was afflicted in every way (2 Corinthians 4:8). Even in the midst of his problems, Paul was not defeated. He was not crushed, nor driven to despair. Because of his faith, the Lord gave him a free drop – a chance to begin again.

Jesus does that today for each of us. He said, "Come to me, all you that are weary and are carrying heavy burdens and I will give you rest. Take my yoke upon you, and learn from me; for I am gentle and humble in heart, and you will find rest for your souls. For my yoke is easy, and my burden is light" (Matthew 11: 28-30). I find comfort in the offer to drop my burdens and rely on Jesus. In Him we have hope and the promise of victory. Rejoice!

Indeed, we felt that we had received the sentence of death so that we would rely not on ourselves but on God who raises the dead. He who rescued us from so deadly a peril will continue to rescue us; on him we have set our hope that he will rescue us again. 2 Corinthians 1:9-10

Mulligans

Hit a bad shot? Just take a mulligan and replay the stroke. That sounds impossible, but it sometimes is true. A mulligan is a retaken shot with the first shot not counted. It is granted by an opponent in informal play after a poor shot, especially a drive taken from the tee.

A mulligan is an opportunity to take a shot over; but, a mulligan is never legal under the *The Rules of Golf*. Mulligans are most often allowed during friendly rounds by golf buddies or during charity tournaments when a given number of mulligans may be purchased. Most commonly, mulligans are used only on the first tee or one mulligan may be granted per nine holes.

We are blessed because God understands we sometimes "hit bad shots" in life. That happens when we fail to live up to the standards that God has established. When we "miss the mark" and sin, God gives us an opportunity to take a mulligan. If we repent of our sin, in His mercy He promises to forgive the sin and give us a second chance.

Unfortunately, that does not mean we are free from all penalties of sin. We will suffer consequences but, if we truly repent, God exercises His forgiveness by wiping that sin away, as though it never happened. As God told the Israelites, "I have swept away your transgressions like a cloud, and your sins like mist; return to me, for I have redeemed you" (Isaiah 44:22).

We worship the God of the mulligan. The good news is that He is better than our best golf buddy. He will grant us a mulligan whenever we ask as His love is everlasting and His forgiveness unlimited. Each time we sin, we can repent and ask for His forgiveness. This, however, is no free pass for licentiousness and lawlessness. As Jesus told the Samaritan woman at the well, "Go your way, and from now on do not sin again" (John 8:11).

While we should be grateful for God's patience, everlasting love and forgiveness, our goal should be to no longer need to request any more mulligans.

If we say that we have no sin, we deceive ourselves, and the truth is not in us. If we confess our sins, he who is faithful and just will forgive us our sins and cleanse us from all unrighteousness. 1 John 1:8-9

Rake Bunkers After Use

After taking sand shots, all players should smooth the sand's surface, leaving no signs of divots or footprints and no excess sand on the bunker's edge. For the benefit of subsequent golfers, the sand should be left in as good or better condition than that in which it was found.

When you finish raking a bunker, should you place the rake inside or outside? If placed outside the bunker, the rake could bank a ball onto the sand (or prevent it from falling onto it), but placed inside it could keep a ball on the sand or cause the ball to bury under the rake. What's the rule? There is no rule!

So, what about the rake? If the course has a policy, put the rake where stated. If not, USGA recommends that "on balance it is felt there is less likelihood of an advantage or disadvantage to the player if rakes are placed outside of bunkers." The rake is best placed outside a bunker, parallel to the direction of play on that hole.

It was one of those days. I was on the third hole and my ball hit a rake and ricocheted into a bunker for the third time in the round. So often golf is exasperating and things don't seem to be going right. I approached the sand trap and there was my ball resting in an unraked, shoe-mark depression left by a previous inconsiderate golfer. I had to hit my ball out of a rut created by someone else that never should have been there in the first place.

Our lives, also, are not just about ourselves, but about how we relate to others. We should not live just to meet our needs while at the same time being unaware of the needs of others. Strive to make life better for them. We do not live our lives in isolation. Thomas J. Watson, CEO of IBM, was correct saying, "Really big people are, above everything else, courteous, considerate and generous - not just to some people in some circumstances – but to everyone all the time."

Jesus was asked which commandment of the law is the greatest. He answered, "'You shall love the Lord your God with all your heart, and with all your soul, and with all your mind.' This is the greatest and first commandment. And a second is like it: 'You shall love your neighbor as yourself'" (Matthew 22: 37-39). Whether it is raking a bunker or helping someone in need, we should be aware of how our actions affect others and treat them as well as we treat ourselves.

Let each of you look not to your own interests, but to the interests of others. Philippians 2:4

Lost Cell Phone

After completing my last hole in a golf tournament and returning to the clubhouse, I discovered my cell phone was missing. I had used it on the 12th hole and placed it in a front compartment of the golf cart. Thinking that the phone must have bounced out of the cart, my tournament partner and I returned to that hole and retraced our playing path through the 18th hole. He dialed for my cell phone while we searched. We neither saw nor heard the phone and returned to the clubhouse. I inquired and was told that no one had turned in a cell phone.

About 30 minutes later, my wife suggested I look again while she called the number. I did so and on the on the last hole that I had played, I finally heard the ring and saw the phone glinting in the receding sunlight. I was thrilled and returned to the clubhouse, sharing the good news – rejoicing in what was found.

This incident of lost and found reminded me of Jesus' parables about the lost sheep, the lost coin and the lost son. In every example, the owner or father was grieved at the loss and, then, jubilant and filled with much joy at the recovery of each loss.

Jesus concluded the parable of the lost coin by saying, "Just so, I tell you, there is joy in the presence of the angels of God over one sinner who repents" (Luke 15:10). In reaction to the return of his wayward son, the father said, "But we had to celebrate and rejoice, because this brother of yours was dead and has come to life, he was lost and has been found" (Luke 15:32).

We are lost and separated from God in sin until we acknowledge and repent of our sins, believe in Jesus as our Savior and follow Him. Then, our having returned to the Father, there is rejoicing in heaven for each of us!

From God's perspective, we are much more valuable than my cell phone. Like the phone, we do not realize we are lost. But, God keeps ringing for us and persistently seeks us through the promise of Jesus Christ. When we respond in faith, God rejoices. I felt that in a small way when I found my cell phone and celebrated.

What woman having ten silver coins, if she loses one of them, does not light a lamp, sweep the house, and search carefully until she finds it? Luke 15:8

Fore!

In the middle of the 17th fairway as I prepared to hit my second shot, I heard, "Fore!" I crossed my hands over my head, ducked, and listened for the sound of a ball hitting the ground. With three parallel fairways, an errant ball could be approaching from any direction.

A golfer should shout "Fore!" when it is possible that a golf ball may hit other players or spectators. The term meaning "look ahead" may have come from the military meaning "beware before," which an artilleryman before firing would yell to alert nearby infantrymen to seek cover to avoid the shells coming overhead.

Another explanation could be from the expensive nature of the earliest golf balls. Golfers hired forecaddies to go ahead of them to spot their ball upon landing, similar to how tournaments today employ spotters. After hitting, golfers called out "forecaddie!" to alert him that the ball was coming. Over time, the shout was shortened to "Fore!"

We like to have warning of what is coming, whether it is an event of danger or great anticipation. If the president or a rock star is coming to our city, we want to know when and where that person will arrive. So it was with the Jews in the first century. They anticipated the arrival of the Messiah, their savior. No one knew what he would look like and they were besieged by imposters claiming to be the Messiah.

God called "Fore!" by sending a messenger to proclaim the arrival of the true Messiah. In the wilderness around the Jordan River, John, son of Zachariah, proclaimed a baptism of repentance for the forgiveness of sin. He was the "forecaddie," warning what people must do to receive the Messiah, the one foretold by the prophet Isaiah (40:3-5) who heard a voice cry out, "Prepare the way of the Lord."

Those who pay attention to John's words and respond gain great reward just like those who become alert when they hear "Fore!" on the golf course.

As the people were filled with expectation, and all were questioning in their hearts concerning John, whether he might be the Messiah, John answered all of them by saying, 'I baptize you with water; but one who is more powerful than I is coming; I am not worthy to untie the thong of his sandals. He will baptize you with the Holy Spirit and fire.
Luke 3:15-16

The Challenge

Looking Up

Do not to look up until after you hit the ball; keep your eyes on the ball. This is one of the first principles of golf. The swing is a matter of eye/hand co-ordination.

That sounds like a simple thing to do, but sometimes we just can not do it. When we need to make non-routine shots, we want to see where the balls go before we finish our swings. We see them all right – but they inevitably go someplace unintended.

We can tell our minds what to do, but our bodies do not always respond to the command. The cure is to develop confidence in the shot; then, we will have no need to take an early look forward. We can gain such confidence by practicing our swings and our shots until they become routine.

Until we hit the ball, we should keep our eyes down; then, look up to follow the flight path of the ball to its target. When we worship the Lord, we should look up and rejoice in his handiwork. Give thanks to the Lord who "made the sun to rule over the day, for his steadfast love endures forever; the moon and stars to rule over the night, for his steadfast love endures forever" (Psalm 136:8-9).

Look up to the sky. "The heavens tell of the glory of God. The skies display his marvelous craftsmanship" (Psalm 19:1). The creation, power and presence of God are evident in the heavenly bodies which display evidence of the existence and power of God for all to see merely from the observation of nature.

Look up and enjoy what God has created but do not worship those heavenly objects or anything else of creation. Worship God alone for he has chosen those who believe in him as His own and redeemed us through the sacrifice of his Son Jesus Christ. Give thanks to God for his mercy and steadfast love.

And when you look up into the sky and see the sun, moon, and stars—all the forces of heaven—don't be seduced by them and worship them. The LORD your God designated these heavenly bodies for all the peoples of the earth. Remember that the LORD rescued you from the burning furnace of Egypt to become his own people and special possession; that is what you are today. Deuteronomy 4:19-20

The Woods

I have never seen a golf course without trees. Many have groves of trees or just plain woods. Pines and palms may be found near the coast and hardwood trees further inland. Mountain courses may have both evergreen and deciduous trees. Hopefully, when and where we play, the woods near the fairways have been thinned and the ground groomed.

Occasionally our balls find their way into those woods when we hit bad shots or misjudge our shots. Then, we must try to find a clear path to shoot the ball back into the fairway; otherwise, we declare an unplayable lie or a lost ball, take a penalty stroke and place a ball back into play. When we end up in the woods because of our errors, we have a price to pay.

Tiger Woods has struggled to get out of the "woods." On November 15, 2009, he won the Australian Masters in Melbourne for his 82nd career victory. Twelve days later, he drove his SUV into a tree near his Florida home, setting off shocking revelations that he had been cheating on his wife. The resulting sex scandal cost Woods his marriage, over two years with no tour wins and the loss of advertising contracts and endorsements.

Recovering his golf game in the midst of his moral indiscretions has proven to be challenging. He was not again in contention to win a tournament until December 5, 2010, at his own Chevron World Challenge. In the playoff, Graeme McDowell made a 25 foot putt to beat Woods. Finally after 924 days, he won a PGA golf tournament, the Arnold Palmer Invitational at Bay Hill on March 24, 2012.

Once in the woods, it is not easy to get out without a penalty. With moral and ethical transgressions, it is impossible. In the game of life, the Lord has provided us with his commandments and ordinances to guide our behavior. When we follow those precepts, we avoid sinning and stay out of trouble. When we violate his guidance, we leave the groomed "fairway" and get into the "woods," bringing trouble upon ourselves.

Long ago, a psalmist observed, "Trouble and anguish have come upon me, but your commandments are my delight" (Psalm 119:143). For life without penalties, we need to commit to follow the precepts of the Lord and stay out of the "woods."

Better is a little with the fear of the Lord than great treasure and trouble with it. Proverbs 15:16

The Lost Ball

No matter the caliber of a golfer, inevitably, all golfers may lose one or more balls on the course in a round. One of the great universal comforts of the game is that even the world's best players lose golf balls.

No one knows exactly how many golf balls are lost worldwide, although it has been estimated that, annually, it may be 300 million in the United States. Hundreds of thousands of golf balls can be lost or abandoned in a single day in lakes, ponds, forests, wetlands, deserts, backyards, gardens, parking lots, cemeteries, on rooftops, over fences, under leaves or in groundhog holes.

"For every lost ball, there was a forlorn search, perfunctory or thorough," John Updike wrote in the foreword to "Lost Balls," a 2005 golf book. Lost balls have created an industry. Lost-golf-ball-retrieval entrepreneurs, amateur and professional, work hard to recover and reclaim millions of golf balls every week. Few lost golf balls will remain in water as long as there are scuba-diving-retrievers.

No ball is ever hit to be lost as every lost ball was once a hopeful shot that went astray. The lost golf ball may be a metaphor for life. We each were created in the image of God, but fell to sin. All of us are lost and waiting to be found. We continue to sin (miss the mark) and stay separated from God. Unlike every golf ball, every one of us becomes lost.

The good news is that God, a retriever entrepreneur, is searching and reaching out for us. Just like the shepherd who searched until he found his lost sheep and the golfer who seeks his lost ball, God steadfastly searches for us. He sent Jesus to die for our sins and when we repent and accept Him, there is joy in the presence of the angels of God in heaven. A golfer may not find his lost ball, but every sinner is known by and has the opportunity to be found and redeemed by God.

Which one of you, having a hundred sheep and losing one of them, does not leave the ninety-nine in the wilderness and go after the one that is lost until he finds it? When he has found it, he lays it on his shoulders and rejoices. And when he comes home, he calls together his friends and neighbors, saying to them, "Rejoice with me, for I have found my sheep that was lost." Luke 15: 4-6

Why Is It So Hard?

Interviewed on The Golf Channel, Bobby Jones' son was asked what his father might think about the state of the game of golf today. He replied, "I think he'd be disappointed that the game had not gotten any easier to learn."

While playing in a Pro-Am tournament, Tommy Armour III commented to me about golf, "It's an easy game to learn, but a hard game to master." I am not so sure it is that easy to learn, but it certainly is difficult to master.

There are many books of instruction on the game of golf and on the USGA's *The Rules of Golf.* There are plenty of golf teachers – some who are superb and others mediocre. Also, fellow golfers often like to give solicited or unsolicited advice. It is fairly simple to learn the basic rules of golf, to stand over the ball and swing the club and make contact with the ball.

To master the game to one's ability level is the challenge. Golf is inherently difficult because of the miniscule margin for error. Most swings are not grooved to nail the sweet spot consistently. Then, golfers must judge the distance, the lay of the land, the wind speed and other factors. Finally, we must be prepared mentally and not expect too much or try

72

to play perfectly. We need to strive to gain confidence, make a good club selection, relax and take the shot.

Like golf, being a Christian is easy to begin and impossible to perfect. The simple part is being saved. Jesus has already paid the price by his sacrifice for our sins on the cross at Calvary. By faith, just say "Yes" to Jesus and accept his offer of eternal salvation. Once we accept Jesus, from our gratitude will come the desire to please Him by living the life Jesus would have us live.

That is the difficult part – to put Jesus' will ahead of our own will and to follow the ways of God, not the ways of the world. Even though we continue to sin and stay self-centered, we increasingly will desire to strive to be more holy – more set apart for God. That is the process of sanctification.

Let's master the Christian life by praying constantly, studying God's word, exerting efforts to do his will and simply persevering.

For by grace you have been saved through faith, and this is not your own doing; it is the gift of God. Ephesians 2:8

Learn From Mistakes

My ball was lying deep in the Bermuda grass rough about 100 yards from the green. I aligned my sand wedge, and took my shot. The grass opened the clubface; the ball flew up to the right and out of bounds. Immediately, I knew I should have used my pitching wedge and opened the face prior to taking the shot. After my penalty stroke, I did just that and landed the ball in the center of the green. Without hesitation, I had analyzed the error of my first shot and learned from my mistake.

One mistake that occurs for many golfers involves the short putt. The ball is stroked lightly and does not roll to the hole. The cure for short putts is found in increasing one's confidence level. When putts consistently are short, we need to strike the ball harder and practice doing so, concentrating on distance control. Just try to get the ball to roll at least one foot beyond the cup.

As with short puts, sometimes we make the same mistake over and over and learn very slowly from our mistakes. The Bible is replete with accounts of the Israelites' sins against God and their backslidings from him. They struggled to learn from their mistakes. Such behavior is typical of the infidelity to God of many Christians today.

We are fortunate to be able to see that God's judgments on the Israelites foreshadow God's current spiritual judgments. Paul recognized and wrote to the Corinthians that future followers of Christ could benefit from understanding the apostasy of certain Jews. Their exclusion from the earthly Canaan typifies the exclusion of many Christians, today, from the heavenly Canaan, for or because of their unbelief. The Hebrew history was written to be an example for today's Jewish and Christian people alike.

We can and should learn from mistakes – ours and others. Nothing in scripture is written in vain. God had wise and gracious purposes for us in leaving the record of Jewish spiritual history. We should use our wisdom, commitment and strength to learn from it.

These things happened to them to serve as an example, and they were written down to instruct us, on whom the ends of the ages have come. 1 Corinthians 10:11

New Clubs

The USGA's *The Rules of Golf* state that no more than 14 clubs, including the putter, are allowed in a golfer's bag during a round of golf. Golfers may have that complete component of clubs but if their scores are increasing, they may think that a new driver, putter, wedge or a set of irons will be just the thing to improve their performances.

Golfers do not enjoy playing badly and have a built-in desire to be good at their endeavors. We may easily believe that new clubs may be necessary to improve our scores.

Golf club manufacturers each year develop new equipment and proclaim that each new club is better than the last, providing more distance and better accuracy. Perhaps new clubs will improve your confidence and be better matched to your swing and present abilities. But, look beyond the propaganda. Read reviews, talk to teaching professionals and try out the clubs.

You may have an old Bible, one passed down from a parent or one received at your confirmation. It may be a King James' Version or a Revised Standard Version, each a translation of the inspired Word of God. You may read it everyday and benefit greatly. Nonetheless, you may improve your understanding by using a Bible with less archaic language and with illuminating footnotes. Consider adding the Common English Bible or The New Oxford Annotated Bible containing the New Revised Standard Version.

Just as golfers can play with old clubs or new ones, Christians can receive the Word of God through older and newer translations of the Bible. One does not preclude the other, but newer translations in contemporary language may improve our understanding of God's message. "For whatever was written in former days was written for our instruction, so that by steadfastness and by the encouragement of the scriptures we might have hope" (Romans 15:4).

Unlike the limit on our golf clubs, the number of Bibles we can use is unlimited. We can become familiar with several translations of the Bible and use each to augment our understanding of God's Scriptures.

All scripture is inspired by God and is useful for teaching, for reproof, for correction, and for training in righteousness.
2 Timothy 3:16

The Mind

Controlling Emotions

Golfing elicits emotions. One reason to play the game is to experience the joy of victory; but, it also can deliver the agony of defeat. Discrete, short-lived emotions can come to the fore during our rounds when we experience feelings of joy, anger or disgust.

After several poor shots, a golfer may feel anger and negativity. In that instant the sport is no longer fun, and if the golfer doesn't control his emotions, they will control him. Confucius said, "When anger rises, think of the consequences." W. Clement Stone, a rags-to-riches businessman and self-help book author who died in 2002 at the age of 100, said "When we direct our thoughts properly, we can control our emotions." Overcoming emotions can be challenging while playing golf but is necessary.

Emotions happen. What is important is how we respond to them. It is normal to show emotion after both good and bad shots; nonetheless, we should not dwell on each feeling. Everyone will be disappointed after hitting the golf ball poorly and will be pleased with great shots. That's fine, but letting emotions swing wildly will become a distraction.

There are ways to limit the variability of emotions, such as developing a routine to use before each shot to concentrate on the next one. Also, we can subordinate emotions to the development of our golf skills to increase our effectiveness or just play the game to be relaxed and have a good time.

The book of Proverbs transmits wisdom to show people how to cope with life and their emotions. The proverbs are guided by the overarching principle that "the fear (reverence) of the Lord is the beginning of wisdom" (Proverbs 1:7; 9:10; 15:33). In Proverbs, wisdom, generally equated with righteousness, brings success while wickedness leads to destruction.

Just as in golf we use "How To" books and golf magazines to learn more about the sport of golf, in life we use the Bible to learn more about God and ourselves. Read and meditate upon the wisdom of Proverbs. Let's rely on God's Word and control our emotions.

Those with good sense are slow to anger, and it is their glory to overlook an offence. Proverbs 19:11 *A violent-tempered person will pay the penalty.* Proverbs 19:19a

Calm Under Pressure

In the 2011 Masters at the Augusta National Golf Club , 21-year-old Rory McIlroy from Northern Ireland had a four-shot lead going into the final day but blew almost all of it on one disastrous hole. He finished the tournament 10 shots behind Charl Schwartzel for a tournament total of four under par. "Well, it's going to be hard to take for a couple of days," McIlroy said after shooting an eight-over-par 80 on Sunday. "But I'll be O.K. I didn't see it coming even though I know it's happened before. It's very disappointing." Such is the result of buckling under pressure.

Charl Schwartzel from South Africa won that 75th Masters with birdies on the final four holes, finishing with the day's low round of 66 for a tournament total 14-under-par 274. He prevailed through a chaotic afternoon shootout in which eight golfers at one time or another shared in the lead. Never before had a Masters champion birdied the last four holes in a final round.

If ever there is pressure in golf it will be found in the final day on the back nine in a major golf tournament. How a golfer counters such pressure becomes a major determinant in the final outcome of any tournament. McIlroy and Schwartzel responded very differently to such intense pressure.

We face pressure in many ways and from many sources. There can be stress from work and play, friends and foes, strangers and family, and even ourselves. Stress is a normal part of life. But, too much stress can lead to emotional, psychological, and physical problems -- including heart disease, high blood pressure, chest pains, or irregular heartbeats. Chronic stress exposes our bodies to unhealthy, persistently elevated levels of adrenaline and cortisol.

In times of stress, we should follow Paul's advice to the Philippians and turn to God in prayer asking through Jesus for strength, wisdom and confidence to endure the pressure. When we place our trust in Jesus, he is always with us and provides the comfort we need. We will not always win the match but we will be comforted by the King of kings.

Do not worry about anything, but in everything by prayer and supplication with thanksgiving let your requests be made known to God. And the peace of God, which surpasses all understanding, will guard your hearts and your minds in Christ Jesus.
Philippians 4:6-7

Snapping Back

Do you try to keep deeply focused on golf throughout the entire round? Do you concentrate so hard that your energy is totally drained by the end of the match? Or do you have a way of mentally withdrawing and relaxing after a shot, then snapping back into focus for the next shot?

Snapping back involves relaxing between shots and thinking about the next shot only when planning it and beginning your pre-shot routine. Planning a shot includes selecting the target spot, judging the distance, evaluating the wind and selecting the club. The pre-shot routine entails visualizing the path of the ball or recalling the feel of the shot, taking a practice swing, and addressing the ball.

The ability to snap back depends on the golfer's capacity to refocus and let go of unnecessary thoughts, images or feelings. Some people can let their minds wander far away from the scene and still snap back to the shot at hand. Others find it hard to think of anything other than the next shot.

Learn to select energizing, positive or enjoyable thoughts during your time between holes. Between shots, many golfers do best by staying mentally close to the current situation. But even here, we can talk to others, recall a song or think about a really great time playing in the past. We only need to concentrate on playing when we are gathering information, completing our pre-shot routine and executing a shot or putt.

Likewise, we do not have to focus on seeking God every minute of every day worried or concerned as to whether God is with us. We can be calm because we know that his steadfast love endures forever. We can be in contact with God in prayer throughout every day without focusing on God every minute. No matter where we are, God is there.

When we seek Him, in distress or in praise, the Lord is always present and is our salvation. Relax. We can pursue our lives of challenges, routine and celebrations without concern that we will be alone. Jesus, our strength and salvation, is continually with us forever.

Praise the Lord, all you nations! Extol him, all you peoples! For great is his steadfast love towards us, and the faithfulness of the Lord endures for ever. Praise the Lord! Psalm 117

Personal Responsibility

Golf is a game of individual performance – each golfer playing against the field. To attain success, the player must be in good physical condition, use the appropriate equipment, employ consistent swing mechanics and be mentally sharp. Otherwise, his or her game breaks down and the score goes up. There are many organizations and individuals that offer help to a player who wishes to improve his game. They can analyze and suggest but in competition the golfer must execute as an individual.

A player may be the offspring of a professional golfer or of a non-athlete but that does not dictate his level of performance. Each individual must take personal responsibility and develop the skills, fitness and mental strength necessary for peak achievement. Charles Dickens said, "Man blames fate for other accidents, but feels personally responsible when he makes a hole-in-one." We might like to blame others or fate for our shortcomings but the truth is we each have some responsibility for our successes and failures.

We have the same individual responsibility for our spiritual lives. "For we must all appear before the judgment seat of Christ, so that each one may receive what is due for what he has done in the body, whether good or evil " (2 Corinthians 5:10). We each sin and fall short of God's standards; so, we can not rely on what our parents have done or expect our spouse or friends to carry us.

To be our best we become spiritually strong by studying and meditating on the Scriptures, strengthening and maintaining a strong prayer life, and manifesting our faith through acts of love to our neighbors. John Wesley called those activities acts of piety and mercy.

We are individually responsible for our actions and their consequences. That might seem to be a heavy burden; but, God has provided the means for each of us to be reconciled to Him. Accept Jesus as your personal Lord and Savior and you will score your life hole-in-one.

The soul who sins shall die. The son shall not suffer for the iniquity of the father, nor the father suffer for the iniquity of the son. The righteousness of the righteous shall be upon himself, and the wickedness of the wicked shall be upon himself. Ezekiel 18:20

Getting Mad

It happens in an instant. I swing the club, make a mistake and get mad – at myself! I know better than that and can do better than that. Why didn't I keep my eyes on the ball? Why did I not finish my swing? Why did I line up in the wrong direction? It may be one of those or a dozen other issues that result in an errant shot. Getting mad is no solution and is a pretty lame thing to do over a golf shot; nonetheless, it happens.

Everyone gets angry on the course at one time or another, some even to the point of throwing their clubs, a potentially destructive behavior both to the golfer and his playing partners. I deliberately used "his" here as a "he" is usually the culprit. (If you are going to throw a golf club, at least throw it forward so you don't have to go back for it.)

Why do we get frustrated on the golf course? It's actually quite simple; we expect more from ourselves than we deliver. We come under pressure from others or ourselves and become inconsistent in our behavior and swing mechanics. We humans have faults and flaws that show up under pressure. "One given to anger stirs up strife, and the hothead causes much transgression" (Proverbs 29:22). Try not to give in to the impulse of anger.

Just after Peter was given the divine illumination that Jesus is the Messiah, Jesus began to teach that he must undergo great suffering and be killed but would rise after three days. Peter, not wanting to hear such negativity, rebuked Jesus. Then, in front of the disciples Jesus admonished Peter for his self-centered human focus.

Just like Peter, our vision and understanding can change in a minute. We may think that we see clearly but we do not when we focus on what we want rather than seeing through the prism of God. We should not be distracted and upset by insignificant things like an errant golf swing. Instead, we should focus on what is meaningful to God. Listen to the words of Jesus, understand who he is and believe his promises that will lead us to contented lives here and through eternity.

But turning and looking at his disciples, he rebuked Peter and said, "Get behind me, Satan! For you are setting your mind not on divine things but on human things." Mark 8:33

Profanity

Why is golf called golf? Because all the other four-letter words were taken. Profanity is heard on the golf course.

During the third round of The Masters in April 2010, Tiger Woods repeatedly cursed at himself loudly enough for the television microphones to pick it up. His frustrations occurred when Woods made three bogeys in four holes.

After an errant shot on the 6th hole, Tiger closed his eyes in disgust and loudly said, "Tiger Woods, you suck." He continued with a Commandment-breaking expletive. Announcer Verne Lundquist observed, "I don't think he's pleased." All of us can relate to periods of frustration when we function below our expected level of performance.

According to research by Professor Richard Stephens of Keele University in Staffordshire, UK, "swearing elicits an emotional response known as 'stress-induced analgesia,' more commonly known as 'fight or flight,' and with that comes a spurt of adrenalin." That helps one tolerate pain until the pain-causing situation is relieved.

We don't swear because we're mad but because we want to feel good. But, that does not always work. The study discovered that people who swear frequently derive less benefit from swearing when in pain, since the curse words no longer represent a true emotional response. Those who swear regularly and often seem to find no adrenalin benefit at all.

Societies do not desire or condone swearing. Using the name God or Jesus to swear is particularly egregious. It violates one of the Ten Commandments. God is holy – apart and above all His creation – and jealous for His honor. God prohibits the misuse of the divine name in rash or false swearing and is not to be called on lightly or mocked. He is the Lord and expects creation to show reverence and affection to him. Only use the name of God in a serious manner and with an awe of the greatness of His majesty. God, himself, will avenge those who misuse his name.

At times, we each become frustrated with our play and can become exasperated. If we must swear to let off steam and ease the pain, "Golf" is a perfectly acceptable four-letter word to scream on the course!

You shall not make wrongful use of the name of the Lord your God, for the Lord will not acquit anyone who misuses his name.
Exodus 20:7

Watch Out for Alligators

I was on the Ocean Course at The Sea Pines Resort, the first golf course built on Hilton Head Island, SC. Playing this course, featuring strategically placed lagoon and bunkers, is a fabulous experience for both scratch golfers and high handicappers since it is a Certified Audubon Cooperative Sanctuary. This was a family outing and I was sharing the golf cart with my nine-year-old grandson, Cole.

The seventeenth fairway is bordered by a lagoon on the right and out of bounds on the left. Cole hit an approach shot in the direction of the lagoon and the ball came to rest on the shore. As I headed the cart toward the ball, we spotted an alligator sunning itself some forty yards behind the ball. I told Cole I would park near the lagoon and retrieve the ball. I stopped the cart between the gator and the ball and rescued the ball. On my return to the cart, I noticed another gator about thirty yards in front of me. I jumped into the cart and we scurried away. If I had seen both gators first, I would have left the ball for others to find later. Cole took a penalty stroke, dropped the ball and continued to play the hole.

Sometimes on the course of life we come across "alligators," sinful behaviors we should avoid or approach very cautiously. We may be tempted to follow the "way of the wicked" skirting the edge of sinful behavior. We may believe that we can go to the brink and stop before engaging in behavior we know to be wrong. But, life is replete with unseen "alligators." They may lie dormant for the moment, but they can spring to life in an instant and snare us before we know it. The smart and safe approach is to avoid such situations altogether.

If our ball, i.e. our action, leads us into trouble, accept the lost ball and take the penalty. Remaining in the hazard and attempting to retrieve the ball can exacerbate the danger. Retreat from opportunities to engage in sinful behavior. The consequences will be less painful than being led into a fight with an alligator. Avoid the path of the wicked and move on.

Do not enter the path of the wicked, and do not walk in the way of evildoers. Avoid it; do not go on it; turn away from it and pass on. Proverbs 4:14-15

The Successes

The Cup

The objective of the game of golf is to put the ball into the cup with as few strokes as possible. It's amazing and thrilling to do it with a hole-in-one. We may do it with a par, a triple boogie or even more. But, each hole is not finished until the ball drops into the cup.

The standard golf cup is four-and-one-quarter inches in diameter and four inches deep, a courtesy of the Royal and Ancient Golf Club of St. Andrews, Scotland. In its "new" 1891 rules, the R&A determined that a cup of that size should be standard on golf courses everywhere. Where did the standard originate?

A greens keeper at Musselburgh (now a 9-hole municipal course on the Levenhall Links near Edinburgh) in 1829 had invented the first known hole-cutter. The ancient hole-cutter is on display in the clubhouse at the relocated Royal Musselburgh, an 18-hole course in Prestonpans, Scotland. According to legend, the tool was built from excess pipe found on the Musselburgh links.

The objective of the Christian is to accept God's gift of salvation and dwell in the presence of God for eternity. Our citizenship, our ultimate destination, is in heaven with Jesus Christ where "He will transform the body of our humiliation so that it may be conformed to the body of his glory, by the power that also enables him to make all things subject to himself" (Philippians 3:21).

Jesus said he would provide a spring of spiritual water that will give eternal life immediately to those who believe and they will pass from death to life. Those who believe in Him on earth have entered the kingdom of God and while they must continue to live their earthly lives no one can snatch that away from them.

"Jesus said to Martha, 'I am the resurrection and the life. Those who believe in me, even though they die, will live, and everyone who lives and believes in me will never die. Do you believe this?'" (John 11:25-26). Just like Martha, to end the game of life in the cup, we can each accept Jesus and answer, "I believe you are the Messiah, the Son of God."

I press on towards the goal for the prize of the heavenly call of God in Christ Jesus. Philippians 3:14

Gimme

A gimme is a putt that the other players agree can count as made without actually being played. This assumes that the putt would not have been missed. The traditional length of a gimme is within two feet, "within the leather" of a traditional putter. Gimmes are not allowed by the rules in stroke play, but they are often accepted in casual matches.

In match play, either player may formally concede a stroke, a hole, or the entire match at any time, and this may not be refused or withdrawn. A player in match play will generally concede a tap-in or other short putt. A match-play player may concede his opponent's next stroke at any time, as long as his opponent's ball is not moving (Rule 2-4). At that point, the opponent is considered to have holed out.

Accepting gimmes is fine in a social round of golf, but not in stroke play competition. The USGA's *The Rules of Golf* for stroke play require that each golfer continues play until the ball is in the hole. The golfer can be disqualified upon picking up his ball, if he doesn't replace the ball, add the appropriate one-stroke penalty and complete the hole (Rule 18-2 i).

It is joked that a gimme can best be defined as an agreement between two golfers, neither of whom can putt very well. That may be true, but the gimme is an opportunity to treat your opponent as you would like to be treated, an application of the Golden Rule.

Many prominent religious figures and philosophers have stated the bilateral nature of the ethic of reciprocity or the Golden Rule in various ways. It is a basic human right in which each individual is entitled to just treatment and is reciprocally responsible to ensure justice for others.

Jesus' statement in Matthew 7:12, however, is different from all others in that it requires a person to do something favorably to others, while the alternative statements only prohibit persons from doing something unfavorably to others. All that is required is that you don't harm other people. With Jesus, what is required is that you show kindness to others. Giving a gimme putt to your opponent is an offer of kindness. May you sink your long putts and be kind to others!

In everything do to others as you would have them do to you; for this is the law and the prophets. Matthew 7:12

The Perfect Fairway Lie

"Play it as it lies" is one of the basic rules of golf. Much of the time, the golf ball lies in less than a perfect spot – in the rough, in a divot or on a hillside above or below the golfer's stance. It may even be behind a tree or in a ditch.

A golfer may get great satisfaction by hitting a long drive straight down the middle of the fairway and, upon arriving at the ball, find it resting on level terrain cushioned by well-groomed grass – the perfect lie. It's ready for the next brilliant shot and everything is going well.

The next shot may be a good one, landing on the green on a par four hole. Or, even hit well, it may come to rest in a divot which had not been repaired. The golfer moves from a state of bliss to one of disappointment. There is a need to recover when trouble comes, whether or not we are at fault.

Job was a blameless and upright man who feared God and turned away from evil. He was quite prosperous and "the greatest of all people in the east." But, one day without warning, his children were killed and most of his possessions were destroyed. The next day he was afflicted with loathsome sores. His wife implored him to curse God. But Job did not.

Some friends assumed that he had done wrong and offended God. But Job knew he had not. He accepted that God was in control and His goodness would prevail. In the end, it did and the Lord restored Job's possessions and his fortune and blessed him with an expanded family.

Just when things in our lives are going well is the time we may be struck with the unexpected and become subject to a personal disaster or a time of trial. We should prepare for such challenges by building our relationship with the Lord so that during such times we, like Job, can persevere through the trials and emerge ever stronger with God.

The Lord is our creator and sustainer who hears our prayers and wants the best for us. When we are in communion with God and do his will, we have the hope to experience the perfect lie each day. If instead trouble arrives and we remain faithful to him, we can trust God in his steadfast love to sustain us and be with us forever.

So Satan went out from the presence of the Lord, and inflicted loathsome sores on Job from the sole of his foot to the crown of his head. Job 2:7

Member – Guest

A premier event at many golf clubs is an annual member-guest tournament, providing the opportunity for members to invite guests to their club for golf and other social events. Many golfers like the opportunity to share their club.

Here is how one country club promoted its member-guest tournament. "Host someone you'd like to impress, as the golf is great, the camaraderie is greater, and the party afterwards is the greatest. This event will feature team prizes, 36 holes of golf, kick-off cocktail party (beer, wine and soda included) on Thursday, one light breakfast and two lunches, team goody bags, prizes for men and women closest to the pin, hole-in-one prizes and a great time."

Golfers invite friends to play at their home club because, first of all, they have invested their time, money and, perhaps, voluntary service in a club that is meaningful to them. Secondly, they are comfortable at the club and want to share the experience with others. Thirdly, they care about the persons that they are inviting and want them to benefit from the playing experience. Finally, their friends may decide to join them in membership at the club. These are some of the same reasons we should invite friends to join us at our churches. The benefit to them can be much greater than at a golf club.

Andrew answered the call and became one of Jesus' twelve disciples. He is not as well known as his brother, the more aggressive and impetuous Peter. But, Andrew was an inviter. Along with leading Peter to Jesus (John 1:40-42), he brought the boy with loaves and fish to meet Jesus (John 6:8-9); and brought a number of Greeks at their request before Jesus (John 12:20-22).

After Jesus' resurrection and ascension, Andrew went on missionary journeys throughout the East. While Peter came to represent the church of the West (Rome), Andrew came to symbolize the church of the East (Constantinople). He taught in Byzantium (Istanbul), Thrace (southeast Bulgaria and northwest Turkey), Russia, Epiros (southwest Balkans), and Peloponnese (southern Greece). Andrew reminds us that we are to introduce others to Jesus. How about inviting guests to the church where you are a member?

Andrew first found his brother Simon and said to him, 'We have found the Messiah' (which is translated Christ). He brought Simon to Jesus, who looked at him and said, 'You are Simon son of John. John 1:41-42a

I Shot a Birdie!

Golf is not just a fine walk interrupted. Golfers are on the course, not for a walk in a pastoral setting but, to play the best round possible. They would be thrilled with shooting a hole-in-one on a par 3 or a spectacular eagle (2 under par) on a long par 5; nonetheless, they would be quite happy scoring a number of birdies. No, the golfer is not an ornithologist or a clay pigeon enthusiast. A birdie is a score that is one under par on a single hole.

On a par 4 hole, the golf course designers plan for the golfer to reach the green in two shots and sink the ball on the second putt. The golfer gets a birdie when reaching the green in two and sinking the first putt. A birdie can also be scored by holing out the third shot from off the green – difficult for amateur golfers, but top pros do it quite often. Accumulating numerous birdies in one round is a sign of a highly-skilled golfer.

To score a birdie is to perform to a higher standard than that which is usually expected of us. In life, scoring birdies or better is to perform at God's standards which are higher than those of the world. When we see Christians acting in ways that achieve God's standards, we observe people shooting birdies in their daily lives.

Here are some of the ways each of us may shoot birdies in the game of life. Let love be genuine; hate what is evil. Bless and do not curse those who persecute us. Rejoice with those who rejoice; weep with those who weep. Live in harmony with one another; associate with the lowly, and do not claim to be wiser than we are.

Do not repay anyone evil for evil, but live peaceably with all. Never avenge ourselves. "If your enemies are hungry, feed them; if they are thirsty, give them something to drink" (Romans 12:20a). Simply, overcome evil with good by expressing love for one another.

Do not be conformed to this world, but be transformed by the renewing of your minds, so that you may discern what is the will of God – what is good and acceptable and perfect. Romans 12:2

Captain's Choice

A popular format for a charity fundraising golf tournament is a Scramble, sometimes called Captain's Choice. In this format, each player tees off on each hole. The best of the tee shots is selected and all players play their second shots from that spot. The better of the second shots is determined; then, all play their third shots from that spot, and so on until the ball is holed.

There are many variations of the Scramble. In the "Ambrose," handicaps are used with a fraction of the total handicaps of the foursome serving as one handicap for the group. In a "Florida Scramble," the player whose shot is selected doesn't play the next shot. So, all four players tee off, the best shot is selected, and then only three players hit their second shots. The best second shot is selected and the player whose ball is chosen does not hit the third shot; and so on until the ball is holed.

In Captain's Choice, the captain chooses which ball is the best to play and which balls are unacceptable. In many charity tournaments, fundraising gimmicks are typically added, such as selling mulligans, throws or shots from the forward tees.

When teaching his followers what the kingdom of heaven is like, Jesus used the illustration of hiring laborers to work in a vineyard. The owner hired them at different time throughout the day from 6:00 AM until 5:00 PM. They each accepted work at the wage offered at the beginning of their work. That evening, each was paid the same amount, just as the owner promised each individual. As the "Captain," Jesus, alone, makes the choice of how to treat each of us.

Jesus chooses, but in contrast to Captain's Choice in golf, all can be chosen. Jesus reaches out to each of us. He offers us the opportunity to respond – to choose life and be on the Captain's team. Be like Joshua who proclaimed to the people, "As for me and my household, we will serve the Lord" (Joshua 24:15b).

Am I not allowed to do what I choose with what belongs to me? Or are you envious because I am generous? Matthew 20:15

19th Hole

The "19th hole" is a slang term used in golf referring to gathering after the round at a grill, restaurant, bar or pub on or near the golf course. A standard round of golf has only 18 holes but, when the last putt drops, golfers never seem to ask, "What do we do now?" They tend to migrate to the 19th hole, which is as much a part of golf as the previous 18. It's where you settle up the Nassau or other bets placed during the round and enjoy camaraderie with a drink after the game.

Match tied after 18 holes and nowhere to go but the clubhouse? Kinloch Golf Club in Manakin-Sabot, Virginia, northwest of Richmond, offers a unique alternative. Settle the match on a par-3 that involves a water-carry to a green surrounded by frightening bunkers. Kinloch possesses an attribute that golfers may see more of in the years ahead – a real 19th or "Settle-the-Bet" hole.

At other courses, the playing ends at the green on the 18th hole. The game is done and we players depart the course but our lives are not over.

Ultimately, our lives on earth do end; we are at the end of this round. We each will face death sometime in the future but our lives will not be over. We will go on into eternity –

some to eternal life in the presence of God and others to eternal separation from God.

Each of us who has been introduced to Jesus has a choice – to accept Him as Savior or reject Him. This decision comes with eternal consequences. After our "round" on Earth is finished, Jesus will settle our "bets" with him. He said, "I am the way, and the truth, and the life. No one comes to the Father except through me" (John 14:6).

Believe. Accept Jesus and enjoy the "19th hole of eternal life," a place flowing with the river of life in the presence of God.

Then the angel showed me the river of the water of life, bright as crystal, flowing from the throne of God and of the Lamb through the middle of the street of the city. On either side of the river is the tree of life with its twelve kinds of fruit, producing its fruit each month; and the leaves of the tree are for the healing of the nations. Revelation 22:1-2

Too Much Golf

Can there ever be too much golf? Golfers who must play every day the sun shines and most other days could be addicted. They may be like exercise addicts about whom Ian Cockerill, a sports psychologist at the University of Birmingham in England, said, "Healthy exercisers organize their exercise around their lives, whereas dependents organize their lives around their exercise."

Except for the professionals, golf is only a sport to be enjoyed as a means of exercise, competition and escape from the demands of everyday life. Not only can too much golf distract from other important obligations, responsibilities and relationships, it can be physically unhealthy.

The tour pros do not enter every weekly tournament. "First of all, it's not the four in a row that's the problem," said Phil Mickelson. "For me, it's 10 out of 13 weeks in a row (playing). ... It's very difficult to travel with three kids, but to go to 10 different cities in three months is challenging. It's an individual, not a team sport.

"Look, I mean, we play golf for a living," Mickelson said. "I'm not going to try to tell you that it's tough. ... But what's required to play your best golf is a balance. You have to be fresh mentally and physically."

We all have to be refreshed to perform to our potential and part of that process is establishing and keeping a right relationship with God. Our Creator reaches out to us and has provided us with guidance in maintaining a healthy life. One element of that is to keep time apart for God.

To keep the Sabbath holy means to observe it as a day separated from the others, a time belonging especially to God. The exact day is not important as calendar changes have made it impossible to know whether our seventh day is Saturday or Sunday. As Christians, we keep what we believe is the first day of the week because our Lord came back from the dead on that day. It is a day of renewal, rejoicing and worship for us. Let us use the Sabbath to honor and worship the Lord, rejuvenate ourselves, and focus on the love of God and neighbor.

Remember the Sabbath day, and keep it holy. For six days you shall labor and do all your work. But the seventh day is a Sabbath to the Lord your God; you shall not do any work. Exodus 20:8-10a

Praise The Lord

After winning his first PGA tournament, the 2011 Wyndham Championship in Greensboro, NC, Webb Simpson first expressed thanks to Jesus Christ for being with him in his victory; then, he thanked his parents and wife for their support. He followed that victory by winning the Deutsche Bank Championship two weeks later on September 5 at the TCP Boston course and again expressed thanks to Jesus.

Simpson expresses a depth of faith that many do not posses or hesitate to express in public. If we believe in Jesus, we, too, should proclaim him. It is to our eternal benefit to acknowledge him since he said, "Everyone therefore who acknowledges me before others, I also will acknowledge before my Father in heaven" (Matthew 10:32).

It is right for us to give glory to God who created us and sustains us, particularly in the name of Jesus who suffered and died for our salvation. The author of Hebrews tells us that Jesus is not ashamed to call us brothers and sisters. He quotes Psalm 22:22, "I will tell your name to my brothers and sisters; in the midst of the congregation I will praise you." David, in writing this Psalm that foreshadowed the cross of Jesus, was referring to praise of God the Father. It is fitting that the author of Hebrews applies the same verse to praise to Jesus.

Webb Simpson was right and courageous to give thanks to Jesus after his victory just as David did after his rescue "from the horns of the wild oxen." We should also have faith and trust to praise the Lord in times of trial following the example of the prophet Habakkuk (3:17-18). "Though the fig tree does not blossom, and no fruit is on the vines; though the produce of the olive fails and the fields yield no food; though the flock is cut off from the fold and there is no herd in the stalls, yet I will rejoice in the Lord; I will exult in the God of my salvation."

We play golf for about four hours each round but we can have a relationship to Jesus for eternity. Whether we win or lose our golf match, praise God for his steadfast love that endures forever. Do as Paul charged the Ephesians (5:20) to do, "Give thanks to God the Father at all times and for everything in the name of our Lord Jesus Christ."

I will proclaim your name to my brothers and sisters, in the midst of the congregation I will praise you. Hebrews 2.12

About the Author

Harry Underwood has earned the degree of Doctor of Philosophy in Biblical Studies and has provided lay leadership within Presbyterian and Methodist churches. For more than thirty-five years, he has taught small group Bible studies and Sunday School classes. He and his wife Nancy live and golf in Winston-Salem, North Carolina.

Acknowledgements

Writing and golf are both individual activities; one has to perform them by himself. Nonetheless, they can not be mastered without the help of others. In that regard, I am indebted to those who have helped me in the development of this book of devotionals. My writing colleagues Martha Brown, Rod Brown, Linda Coy-Elmore, Steve McCutchen, Al Perry, and Gene Ruble provided many valuable critiques of each devotional over many months. My twin brother Walter read the book draft and offered numerous astute observations, questions and suggestions. I am grateful to PGA professional John Buczek for his insight into the fundamentals of golf and support of this project. Importantly, I thank the Lord for giving me the inspiration and insight to develop this book as a means to spread the message of the Gospel.

Made in the USA
Columbia, SC
25 June 2020

12265672R00065